HOUGHTON MIFFLIN

Reading

Around Town: Neighborhood and Community

HOUGHTON MIFFLIN

BOSTON

ISBN 0-618-38721-8

5 6 7 8 9 10-BS-12 11 10 09 08 07 06 05

Design, Art Management, and Page Production: Silver Editions.

Contents

Sunshine for the Circus

by Linda Dunlap
illustrated by Sarah Dillard

During winter, this town makes room
for new friends. The circus visits!

Sunshine and beaches make circus
people want to stay and play. Days get
hotter. This means they can practice
and play outside.

1

Circus families work and play. Moms
and dads teach little children. Each person
practices and plays hard.

They practice exciting circus acts.
Cheerful boys turn big cartwheels.
Men swing far up. Arms and hands
reach out and catch. It's the neatest
show!

Other days, circus families choose to rest. Groups make the short trip to Shell Beach.

Moms and dads shop at beach stores. Kids fish, splash, and hunt shells.

4

Circus families spend much time each
day with animals. Horses splash in
water and then shake it off. Three horses
are bigger than the others. The little
horses are the cutest! A man checks each
horse's feet and legs.

The biggest cats do not get baths. The
biggest cats just get brushed and fed.

It's time to feed this lion fresh meat.
Do you think they will brush his teeth?

6

Last night, a loud noise shook this house. A family dashed outside. The moon looked bright. The stars looked brighter.

In a flash, the family knew what they had heard. A loud lion sounded louder than thunder! With the circus in town, life can be exciting!

Mother's Day Parade on Park Street

by Linda Dunlap
illustrated by R.W. Alley

Park Street children love parades.
We look for excuses to plan them.

"Let's plan a Mother's Day parade," said Mick.

"That's great!" Jill exclaimed. "What shall we plan?"

"Let me think," Mick said. Then he shouted, "A pet parade! We will march down Park Street with our pets!"

All the children liked that. Each began to think of ways to show pets.

10

Bess made yellow stockings and
shoes for her pup. First she cut yellow
cloth. Then she stitched it.
   The costume looked great!

Latisha picked buckets of fresh
flowers. She planned to make a flower
sash for her sheep.

Then Latisha yelled, "What a mess!"
She found out that sheep chew flowers!

Latisha made another plan. Her
sheep would march in Dad's old slacks.
Dad was willing to help.

Jill had a pet fish. How could she
show a fish? Fish can't march. Fish
can't dress up.

Jill had an idea. She put a little
mattress in Mick's wagon. Then she
placed the fish bowl on the mattress.
She polished the fish bowl, making
it shine.

Mick had still another problem. Mick's problem was his pet, Chuck Chicken. Chickens will not stay in line for long!

Mick went to the pet shop. Way in back, he found a tiny leash.

"Will you sell me this?" Mick asked Miss Black.

"Yes, I will sell it. Let me put it in a sack," Miss Black added.

Mick could use the leash to lead Chuck Chicken.

On Mother's Day, Park Street children got together. Moms, dads, grandmothers, and grandfathers lined the block.

Nell thumped beats on her drum. Kids and willing pets marched around the block. Groups watched and yelled greetings to passing children.

What a swell Mother's Day parade!

Jay the Mailman

by Melissa Blackwell Burke
illustrated by Tom Stanley

Jay has brought mail to people for
years. Jay checks that everything is in
order. This is Jay's last day.

As Jay stops at shops and homes,
people say nice things.

"You are such a good mailman,"
people say. "It will not be the same
without you. Snow or rain could not
keep you away."

"Such high praise!" laughs Jay. "No,
rain can't stop the mail."

Jay gets handshakes. A cute baby in a
playpen waves. Big dogs wag big tails.

"We will miss you," people say. "Don't
stay away."

At the end of this day, Jay makes his
last stop. He's a bit sad. He puts mail in
the last mailbox. He looks up. It's quiet
and then . . . SURPRISE!

Everyone has been waiting inside for
him.

20

In the back yard, the fun begins.

"Did you guess?" Ed asks.

"No way!" Jay exclaims.

"How will you spend your time now?"
Kay asks.

"I may sail and take train trips," Jay
explains. "I may stay home and play
with my grandchildren. And, I'll check
my mail each day!"

21

Everyone visits and eats until sunset.

"Good luck, Jay the Mailman,"
people say.

Jay waves at them. "Maybe I'll see
you soon."

At home, Jay writes everyone nice
notes. He knows just where he will mail
them.

The next day, it rains. Jay takes his notes to the mailbox. He is not in his mailman clothes. On his way, he meets Ed and Kay.

"And why are you out in this rain?" Kay asks.

"Rain still can't stop the mail!" explains Jay.

Watch Out for Thick Mud!

by Melissa Blackwell Burke

illustrated by Jill Newton

Things were slow that day at Rain Forest 911.

Mitch and Beth were not doing much of anything. Just then, a call came in. Rich picked up the line.

"This is Rain Forest 911. Who is it? Do you need help?" Rich asked.

"This is Josh. Sasha needs help. She's in a pit. She's stuck in thick mud!"

"Help is on the way," Rich said.
"Mitch and Beth will be right there.
Look for them."

"Watch out for thick mud!" Josh
exclaimed.

26

Beth and Mitch grabbed their things
and rushed to help Sasha. When they
got near the mud pit, they spotted Josh
and jumped out of the van.

"Show us the way fast, Josh," Mitch
said.

Josh flew up high to show them the
way. Mitch and Beth ran through the
brush.

When Mitch and Beth got to the mud pit, they were so shocked. Yes, Sasha was stuck in that thick mud. She was stuck head first!

"Rain Forest 911 is here, Sasha," Beth said. "We'll get you out of that thick mud in just a while."

Sasha just made a splash with her trunk.

"Watch out for thick mud!" Josh exclaimed.

Mitch got out ropes and other things.

"What do you think?" Mitch asked.
"Shall we try to pull her out with ropes
or push her out with poles?"

"Let's try both," Beth said. "You use
ropes. We'll use poles."

"Watch out for thick mud!" Josh
exclaimed.

Beth, Mitch, and Josh poked and
pulled.   And then, Sasha went "Whoosh!"
Thick mud splashed everywhere, and
Sasha sat up.

"Watch out for thick mud!" Josh
exclaimed.

"What's going on?" Sasha asked.

"You got stuck in thick mud," Beth
explained.   "So Josh got Rain Forest 911."

"Stuck?" Sasha asked. "Well, thanks very much, but I wish you would have checked with me first. I'm not quite finished with my mud bath."

With that, Sasha flipped back into the thick mud with a splash, splash, splash!

"Watch out for thick mud!" Josh exclaimed.

Mouse's Crowded House

by Becky Ward
illustrated by Beth Buffington

"Ouch," said Mouse Mom. "Who bounced that big ball in this house?" But no one could hear her.

She looked at her children . . . so many mice to count. They were so loud that it sounded like a thousand mice playing in the house!

Mice bounded loudly down the steps.
Mice bounced on the bed. One mouse
played soldier with the lampshade. Mice
left wet towels in the bathroom. They
spilled jam behind the couch. It made
Mouse Mom feel like a grouch.

Suddenly Mouse Mom shouted, "No loud sounds allowed! This house is too crowded. Please, go outside NOW!"

The mice fell silent and looked at Mom's frowning face. Without a sound, they picked up their toys and sadly went outside.

Mouse Mom sat down on the couch.
Her house seemed so peaceful. "This is
exactly what I like," thought Mouse
Mom. "I'll just sit and think."

But it was lonely. Mouse Mom could
only think about her children.

Mouse Mom missed those loud,
playful mice. She looked out her
window. Were they bouncing and
bounding and clowning?

No, that's not what she found! Big
Mouse was reading a story, and the rest
were seated next to him on the ground.

"My, my! How nice!" said Mom proudly. And she kissed each mouse.

Then she said sweetly, "Don't stay outside. Please go back inside and play."

So they crowded back in and joyful sounds filled the house.

Mouse Mom felt glad as she watched her children run and play. "This house is not so crowded," she thought. "Now, this house is just right."

Hooray for Main Street

by Becky Ward   illustrated by Doreen Gay-Kassel

"Ray," said Gail, "do you think this town is nice?"

"It's not bad," said Ray.

"Well, I think it is just plain dull," said Gail with a frown.

41

After thinking for a bit, Ray said, "It does not have to stay that way."

"Explain what you mean," said Gail.

"Well, maybe we can make it nice. We can get everyone to help us fix up Main Street," Ray said.

"I like what you're saying. Let's make a plan!" exclaimed Gail.

42

Gail and Ray got red and blue
crayons and wrote on a big, white
box. They made a nice display for
people in town to read. Ray drew
flowers and Gail wrote the words.

This is what Gail wrote on the box:
*Stop and chat with Gail and Ray. Let's
find a way to make Main Street nice.*

Gail and Ray took the display to
town. The children waited for people
to stop and chat. Gail explained that
they needed paint and nails and tools
and flowers. Ray made a list of names
and wrote down things each person
would bring.

44

The next day, the town started
fixing up Main Street. Moms and dads
sawed and nailed while children
painted and planted. Everyone stayed
and helped until daylight was gone.
Gail and Ray thanked them for helping.

The mayor made Sunday a big day.
He praised the new Main Street with its
rainbow of flowers. He praised Gail and
Ray and those who had helped them.
Then the band played while everyone
marched down Main Street. Gail and
Ray proudly led the way.

"Now this town is very nice," said Ray. "It is not plain or dull."

"I'll say!" exclaimed Gail. "Now this town makes us proud. It is as nice as it can be!"

Then everyone in town stood up and shouted out loud, "Hooray for Main Street! Hip! Hip! Hooray!"

The Clean Team

by Anne Walker
illustrated by Daniel Powers

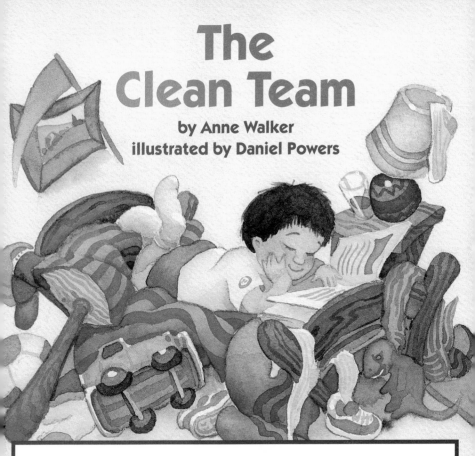

Mike knew he should be cleaning his room.

But he was reading such a good book! It told about a lady who ruled a land near the sea. This queen looked silly but she did lots of neat tricks.

Mike turned the page to read more.

49

Then Mike's mom opened his door.
"Mike, we will leave for the park in
ten minutes," she told him. "The town
cookout starts at noon. You may join us
if your room is clean."

Mike looked around. His room was a
real mess. Toys peeked out from under
his bed. Heaps of jeans lay on the floor.
Pictures he had made were left about.

Mike got down on his knees. He
reached under the bed for a small boat.
Then he heard an odd sound.

"Knock! Knock! Scratch! Scratch!"

51

Mike glanced up. He saw Jean and their dog Queen standing near the door.

"We will help clean your room," said Jean. "We can make cleaning up fun."

"Wow! Thanks, Jean," said Mike.

"We will be a team," said Jean.

"The clean team," said Mike.

Then she and Mike began to clean up the mess. Even Queen got in on the action. When she picked up a ball, Mike said, "Thanks, Queen! You're such a sweet lady!"

53

Soon Mike's whole room was as neat as a pin. Mike could not believe his eyes. "Each toy is away," he said.

"All the furniture is clean," said Jean. "We make a good team!"

54

Mike had fun at the cookout. He ate hot dogs and peach pie. He flew a kite.

But the cookout was not the best part of Mike's day. It was cleaning up with the clean team.

Big Hound's Lunch

by Anne Walker
illustrated by Ilene Richards

Mom handed Anna a sack.

"Please take this sack to Dad. His
lunch is in it," she said.

Anna took the sack and skipped out
of the house.

57

Anna's brown dog bounded up to her.
"It is time to take Dad his lunch, Big
Hound," Anna said. She put a leash on
Big Hound and they set off. Big Hound
took the sack.

58

Mister Trout waved from his mail
truck. Anna waved back. Big Hound
wagged the lunch sack at Mister Trout.

Anna smiled. "Big Hound!" she said.
"That lunch is for Dad!"

Miss Pound sat on her porch.

"Good morning, Anna," she said. She
did not say anything to Big Hound. Big
Hound jumped up and down with the
lunch sack. Anna smiled. "Big Hound!"
she said. "That lunch is for Dad!"

60

Anna and Big Hound passed Tim's house. Tim bounced his ball to Anna. Anna threw it back.

Big Hound didn't play ball. He pounced on the sack. Anna smiled. "Big Hound!" she said. "That lunch is for Dad!"

Anna and Big Hound reached Dad's store. Anna kissed Dad. She said, "Dad! We brought your lunch."

Then Anna saw that Big Hound was eating Dad's lunch. "Big Hound!" she said. "That lunch was for Dad."

"Well," Dad said. "We can go out to eat."

"Great!" Anna shouted. "May we go
to Sprouts? It is our special place."

Big Hound wagged his tail. He loved
to go to lunch.

Word Lists

Sunshine for the Circus (p. 1) accompanies *Chinatown.*

DECODABLE WORDS

Target Skills
Consonant Digraphs *th, wh, sh, ch (tch)*
baths, beach, beaches, brush, brushed, cartwheels, catch, chances, checks, cheerful, children, choose, dashed, each, fish, flash, fresh, much, reach, shake, Shell, shells, shook, shop, short, show, splash, sunshine, teach, teeth, than, then, think, this, thunder, with

Structural Analysis: Base Words and Endings *-er, -est*
bigger, biggest, brighter, cutest, hotter, louder, neatest

Words Using Previously Taught Skills
acts, and, animals, arms, at, be, big, boys, bright, can, cats, circus, dads, day, days, exciting, family, families, far, fed, feed, feet, for, get, groups, had, hands, hard, his, horse's, horses, house, hunt, it, it's, just, kids, knew, last, legs, life, looked, loud, make, makes, man, means, meat, men, moms, moon, new, night, noise, not, out, outside, person, play, plays, practice, practices, rest, rooms, spend, stars, stay, stores, swing, that, three, time, town, turn, trip, up, visits, will, you

HIGH-FREQUENCY WORDS

New
heard, during, lion, winter

Previously Taught
a, are, do, friends, in, little, off, other, others, people, the, they, to, want, water, what, work

Mother's Day Parade on Park Street **(p. 9)** accompanies *Chinatown.*

Target Skill (Review)
Double Consonants
added, back, Bess, Black, block, buckets, Chicken, chickens, Chuck, dress, Jill, mattress, mess, Mick, Nell, passing, picked, sack, sell, shall, slacks, still, stockings, swell, will, willing, yelled, yellow

Words Using Previously Taught Skills
an, and, asked, beats, bowl, can't, chew, children, cloth, costume, cut, Dad, Dad's, dads, day, down, drum, each, exclaimed, excuses, first, fish, for, found, fresh, greetings, groups, had, he, help, her, his, in, it, kids, Latisha, lead, leash, let, let's, liked, line, lined, look, looked, made, make, making, march, marched, me, Mick's, Miss, moms, not, on, out, parade, parades, Park, pet, pets, placed, plan, planned, polished, problem, pup, put, sash, she, sheep, shine, shop, shouted, show, stay, stitched, street, that, that's, them, then, this, think, thumped, up, use, wagon, watched, way, ways, we, went, with, yes

Previously Taught
a, all, another, around, began, could, flower, flowers, grandfathers, grandmothers, great, how, I, idea, little, long, love, Mother's, of, old, our, said, shoes, the, tiny, to, together, was, what, would, you

Jay the Mailman (p. 17) accompanies *A Trip to the Firehouse.*

Target Skills

Vowel Pairs *ai, ay*

day, exclaims, explains, Jay, Jay's, Kay, mail, mailbox, mailman, may, play, playpen, praise, rain, rains, sail, say, stay, tails, train, waiting, way

Compound Words

backyard, grandchildren, handshakes, inside, mailbox, mailman, maybe, playpen, sunset, without

Words Using Previously Taught Skills

and, as, asks, at, be, begins, big, bit, can't, check, checks, cute, did, dogs, don't, each, eats, Ed, end, everything, for, fun, gets, good, has, he's, high, him, his, home, homes, how, I'll, in, is, it, it's, just, keep, knows, last, looks, luck, makes, meets, miss, my, next, nice, no, not, notes, now, on, or, out, puts, sad, same, see, shop, shops, snow, soon, spend, still, stop, stops, such, take, takes, that, them, then, these, things, this, time, trips, until, up, visits, wag, waves, we, why, will, with, writes, years

New

clothes, guess, order

Previously Taught

a, are, away, baby, been, brought, could, he, I, laughs, of, people, quiet, surprise, the, to, where, you, your

Watch Out for Thick Mud! **(p. 25)** *accompanies A Trip to the Firehouse.*

DECODABLE WORDS

Target Skill (Review)
Consonant Digraphs *th, wh, sh, ch, (tch)*
bath, Beth, brush, checked, finished, Josh, Mitch, much, push, Rich, rushed, Sasha, shall, she, she's, shocked, show, splash, splashed, thanks, that, them, then, they, thick, things, think, this, with, when, while, whoosh, wish

Words Using Previously Taught Skills
and, asked, at, back, be, but, came, day, exclaimed, explained, fast, flew, flipped, for, get, going, got, grabbed, help, her, high, I'm, in, into, is, it, jumped, just, line, look, made, me, mud, my, need, needs, not, on, or, out, picked, pit, poked, poles, pulled, quite, ran, rain, right, ropes, sat, she's, slow, so, spotted, stuck, thanks, that, then, trunk, try, up, us, use, van, way, we, well, went, when, while, whoosh, will, wish, with, yes, you

HIGH-FREQUENCY WORDS

Previously Taught
a, anything, call, called, do, doing, everywhere, first, forest, gone, have, head, here, I, is, near, of, other, pull, said, she, the, their, there, they, through, to, very, was, watch, we'll, were, what, what's, who, would

Mouse's Crowded House **(p. 33)** accompanies *Big Bushy Mustache.*

DECODABLE WORDS

Target Skills

Vowel Pairs *ou, ow*
about, allowed, bounced, bouncing, bounded, bounding, clowning, couch, count, crowded, down, found, frowning, grouch, ground, house, how, howling, loud, loudly, mouse, now, ouch, out, outside, proudly, shouted, sound, sounded, sounds, thousand, towels, without

Suffixes *-ly, -ful*
exactly, lonely, sadly, suddenly, sweetly, joyful, peaceful, playful

Words Using Previously Taught Skills
and, as, at, back, bathroom, bed, big, but, children, each, face, feel, fell, felt, filled, glad, go, her, him, in, inside, is, it, jam, just, kissed, knocked, lampshade, left, like, looked, made, mice, missed, Mom, mom's, my, next, nice, no, not, on, picked, play, played, playing, please, reading, rest, right, run, sat, seated, seemed, she, sit, so, spilled, stay, steps, that, that's, them, then, think, this, those, toys, up, went, wet, window, with

HIGH-FREQUENCY WORDS

New
behind, soldier, story

Previously Taught
a, ball, could, don't, hear, I, I'll, many, one, only, said, silent, the, their, they, thought, to, too, was, were, what, who

Hooray for Main Street (p. 41) accompanies *Big Bushy Mustache.*

Target Skill (Review)
Vowel Pairs *ay, ai*
crayons, day, daylight, display, exclaimed, explain, explained, Gail, hooray, Main, maybe, mayor, nailed, nails, paint, painted, plain, played, praised, rainbow, Ray, say, saying, stay, stayed, Sunday, waited, way

Words Using Previously Taught Skills
and, as, bad, band, be, big, bit, blue, box, bring, can, chat, children, dads, down, drew, dull, each, fix, fixing, for, frown, get, got, had, he, help, helped, helping, hip, in, is, it, it's, its, just, led, let's, like, list, loud, made, make, makes, marched, mean, moms, much, names, needed, new, next, nice, not, now, on, or, out, plan, planted, proud, proudly, read, red, sawed, shouted, started, stood, stop, Street, than, thanked, that, them, then, things, think, thinking, this, those, took, tools, town, until, up, us, we, well, while, white, with, wrote

HIGH-FREQUENCY WORDS

Previously Taught
a, after, do, does, everyone, flowers, gone, have, I, I'll, more, of, people, person, said, the, they, to, very, was, what, who, words, would, you, you're

The Clean Team (p. 49) accompanies *Jamaica Louise James.*

Target Skills

Vowel Pairs *ee, ea*

clean, cleaning, each, find, heaps, Jean, jeans, knees, neat, peach, peeked, Queen, reached, read, reading, real, sea, seeds, sweet, team

Common Syllables *-tion, -ture*

action, furniture, pictures

Words Using Previously Taught Skills

about, an, and, around, as, at, ate, away, ball, be, bed, best, big, boat, book, but, can, cookout, day, did, dogs, down, even, flew, floor, for, from, fun, glanced, good, got, had, he, help, him, his, hot, if, in, is, it, join, kite, knew, knock, lady, land, lay, left, looked, lots, made, make, may, mess, Mike, Mike's, mom, more, noon, not, odd, on, out, page, park, part, picked, pie, pin, room, ruled, sack, saw, scratch, she, silly, soon, sound, standing, starts, such, ten, thanks, then, this, told, town, toy, toys, tricks, turned, up, us, we, when, will, with, wow, you, you're

New

believe, lady, whole

Previously Taught

a, all, began, could, door, eyes, heard, minutes, near, of, opened, said, should, small, the, their, to, under, was, were, who, your

Big Hound's Lunch (p. 57) accompanies *Jamaica Louise James.*

Target Skill (Review)
Vowel Pairs *ow, ou*
brown, bounced, bounded, down, Hound, house, our, out, pounced, pound, shouted, sprouts, Trout

Words Using Previously Taught Skills
and, Anna, Anna's, at, back, big, can, Dad, Dad's, day, did, didn't, dog, eat, eating, for, from, go, good, had, handed, he, her, his, in, is, it, jumped, kissed, leash, lunch, mail, may, Miss, Mister, Mom, morning, not, on, passed, past, place, play, please, porch, reached, sack, sat, saw, say, set, she, skipped, smiled, store, tail, take, that, then, this, threw, time, Tim, Tim's, took, truck, up, wagged, waved, we, well, with

HIGH-FREQUENCY WORDS

Previously Taught
a, anything, ball, brought, great, I, loved, of, off, put, said, special, the, they, to, was, your

71

HIGH-FREQUENCY WORDS TAUGHT TO DATE:

Grade 1	buy	five	idea	open	small	watched	kitchen
a	by	flower	in	or	so	water	lady
able	call	fly	is	other	some	we	later
about	car	follow	jump	our	soon	wear	letter
above	carry	for	kind	out	start	were	lion
afraid	caught	forest	know	over	sure	what	move
after	children	found	laugh	own	table	where	order
again	cling	four	learn	paper	talk	who	poor
against	cold	friend	light	part	tall	why	quiet
all	color	full	like	people	teacher	work	reason
already	come	funny	little	person	the	world	roll
also	could	garden	live	picture	their	would	soldier
always	cow	girl	long	piece	there	write	special
and	dance	give	look	play	these	you	stand
animal	divide	go	love	present	they	your	story
any	do	goes	many	pretty	thought		straight
are	does	gone	me	pull	three	**Grade 2**	surprise
arms	done	good	minute	put	through	across	touch
around	door	green	more	read	tiny	beautiful	until
away	down	grow	morning	ready	to	behind	whole
baby	draw	happy	most	right	today	believe	winter
bear	eat	hard	mother	room	together	bought	word
because	edge	have	my	said	too	brother	year
been	eight	he	near	saw	try	brought	young
before	else	head	never	school	turn	busy	
began	enough	hear	not	second	two	clothes	
begin	evening	her	now	see	under	different	
bird	ever	here	ocean	seven	upon	during	
blue	every	hold	of	shall	very	even	
body	fall	horse	off	sharp	walk	floor	
both	family	house	old	she	wall	front	
break	far	how	on	shoe(s)	want	great	
brown	father	hungry	once	shout	warm	guess	
build	find	hurt	one	show	was	heard	
butter	first	I	only	sing	wash	important	

Decoding Skills Taught to Date: Short Vowels *a, i;* Base Words and Endings *–s, -ed, -ing;* Short Vowels *o, u, e;* VCCV Pattern; Long Vowels *a, i* (CVC*e*); Long Vowels *o, u, e* (CVC*e*); Two Sounds for *g;* Consonant Clusters *r, l, s;* Two Sounds for *c;* Double Consonants; VCV Pattern; Final *k* and *ck;* Consonant Digraphs *th, wh, sh, ch, (tch);* Base Words and Endings *–er, -est;* Vowel Pairs *ai, ay;* Compound Words; Vowel Pairs *ow, ou;* Suffixes *–ly, -ful;* Vowel Pairs *ee, ea;* Common Syllables *–tion, –ture*